Total Rewards Communication Handbook

Version 7

A Step-by-Step Guide to Communicating the Full Value of

Employment to Improve Engagement and Retention

TOTAL
REWARDS
COMMUNICATION

IMPROVE EMPLOYEE RETENTION AND
ENGAGEMENT

Total Rewards Communication Handbook

Version 7

A Step-by-Step Guide to Communicating the Full Value of
Employment to Improve Engagement and Retention

Ezra Schneier

March 2017

Total Rewards Communication Handbook, Version 7

March 2017

ISBN 978-1-365-77113-2

Contents

Acknowledgements

Thank you to the colleagues who have generously shared their insights and wisdom to make this project possible. We are indescribably grateful for your suggestions and guidance.

Total Rewards Communication is an effective way to enhance employee retention and engagement.

Building awareness about an employer's values and supporting a company's goals can be achieved with attention to Total Rewards Communication.

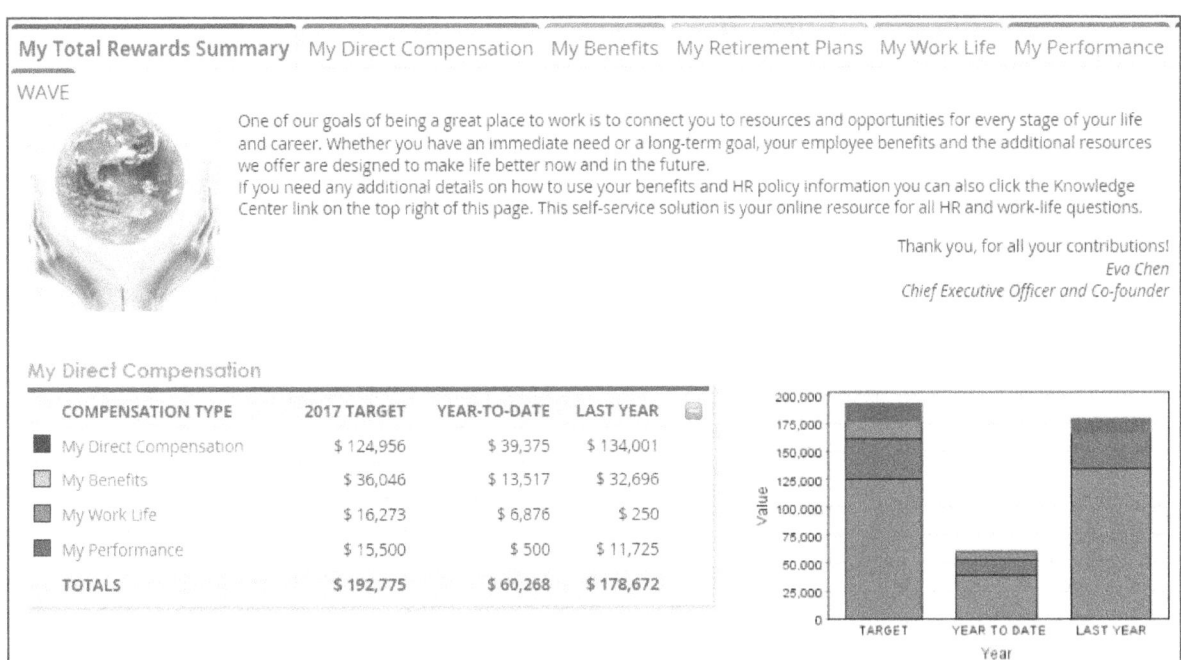

Preface

Routine Total Rewards (TR) Communication is appropriate for most employers.

A proper Total Rewards Communication program can help employers improve business results by having more engaged and better informed associates.

It can take the form of a simple e-mail, a more elaborate statement or an on-line experience. The purpose and message is consistent:

- You are a valued employee. We supply you with this compensation and other benefits in recognition of all you do.

- Here is how our incentive and benefit programs work.

- We want to have an open, candid dialogue about compensation, benefits and employment.

- We are committed to having a strong employer/employee relationship and meet your expectations.

- We value results and believe in Pay for Performance.

Many employers do not have a Total Rewards Communication strategy in place. The purpose of this handbook is to discuss how easy it can be to bring one to your organization. By breaking it down into discreet steps, we hope more employers will develop and implement Total Rewards Communication.

We believe there is a TR Communication plan for everyone. This should not be a one-time event. It should come with a clearly stated purpose and a commitment to ongoing communication.

TR Communication shows the full value of employment. But there is much more.

One last thing: It is tempting for employers to make TR Communication a self-serving message about the company's generosity. That misses a much greater opportunity. The larger picture includes:

- ✓ Enhanced engagement and employee retention.

- ✓ Better alignment of individual efforts and organizational goals.

- ✓ Improved business results.

Introduction

Sharing the full value of employment with associates supports career development, retention and engagement - and helps employers achieve their business goals.

With that in mind, the purpose of this handbook is to provide a guide to bringing total rewards communication to your associates.

Much has been written about the importance of aligning a human capital and rewards strategy with an organization's business strategy. Total Rewards Communication is a way to frequently reinforce that linkage by showing all the valuable elements associated with employment and how they tie to organizational goals and performance. In sum, TR Communication adds transparency.

Employees understand they get a salary and benefits for coming to work. But there can be uncertainty about the full value of employment. And there is often not a convenient way to find that information in a simple, user-friendly way. Total Rewards Communication is the answer.

While the specific TR information communicated and the method of sharing can vary, we believe every employer has the ability to have some form of Total Rewards Communication. Our goal here is to help make that happen.

Let's get started.

1: What is Total Rewards Communication?

Total Rewards Communication is a way to improve the relationship between employers and employees.

This communication shares with an associate the value of working for the employer during a specific period of time in the past – and can provide a look into the future.

What's more, TR Communication allows employees to more clearly understand how their incentive program works and see the value of retirement savings plans and health care benefits. Employers use TR Communication as a way to engage employees. It is not just a list of financial items. Rather it is a way to express and reinforce the company's strategy about talent, compensation, pay for performance and rewards.

Total Rewards information can be delivered on a statement (printed or electronic form) or with a full online experience - a personalized web site or portal. In this handbook we will look at both delivery methods. The online method is preferred since it allows for the presentation of current data (and it is how employees want to receive information.) It also gives greater flexibility and the ability for easier personalization. Most of what is presented here can apply to either method of communication.

The benefits of Total Rewards Communication can be summarized this way:

- Restates and reinforces the value of people to the success of an organization.

- Provides a clear message on human capital investments and their alignment with business strategies and goals.

- Challenges the notion of the competitor's "grass is greener..."

- Helps dissuade entitlement if properly implemented.

- Provides a discussion framework for managers to value their employees.

We like to think of TR Communication as the "central hub" for information about compensation, benefits and other items associated with employment. Besides aggregating the full financial value of employment, associates find it useful to have one convenient place to go to find this information. We have all struggled with looking for log-in information for different web sites and managing multiple passwords and user IDs. A central hub eliminates this pain, as far as Total Rewards goes.

With Total Rewards, we consider all the elements – monetary and non-monetary – that are used by an employer to attract, engage and retain associates. Total Rewards has a meaningful impact on the culture of an organization and the employer's talent strategy and business strategy.

As a general rule, rewards include: compensation, benefits, work-life matters, insurance, retirement savings, employee recognition, performance-related remuneration and career development opportunities.

As we plan the Total Rewards Communication, we will always try to think about two key items:

- *How does this reinforce our stated goals for TR Communication?*

- *What advantage does an employee receive?*

In our experience with planning, implementing and supporting these solutions, we see firsthand how employees embrace Total Rewards Communication. The Return on Investment is substantial. The value of this type of communication can also be captured in ways that may not be obvious at first. But some of the benefits include:

- Support for Manager One-on-One Discussions with Associates. Using the Total Rewards Content as a Reference

- Announcing Open Enrollment and Benefits Information/Changes

- Describing Work-Life Benefits

- Highlighting and Reinforcing the Employer's Strategic Goals

- Management Messages

- Learning and Career Development Opportunities.

2: Considerations in Total Rewards

We have broken down the Total Rewards Communication project into separate points to consider. In the following chapters we will discuss each of the items which are summarized below. Of course, every point is not relevant for all employers. But if you choose those items that do pertain to your situation, we hope it will help organize the scope of a solution that meets your desires.

a. Setting Your Goals. Clearly convey to management and associates why the Total Rewards Communication is in place. That is, to easily and directly show the full value of employment, to enhance engagement and to give associates a convenient, useful resource. Establish a clear goal or set of goals for your TR Communication.

b. Choosing the Elements to Include. In this step, the logical categories of rewards are determined and then the specific items within each category are selected. Compensation, Incentive Pay, Retirement Savings, Health Benefits, Continuing Education, Charitable Giving, Work-Life Benefits, etc.

c. Design Phase. After the right data elements and categories are selected for presentation, the next step is to come up with the design and layout of the statement or web site. This is how it will appear to associates. Employers may want to include a brief description about the different elements presented. Also, determine the words used to describe the items (example: "Salary" or "Compensation," "Bonus" or "Incentive Pay.") And what values will be shown: Current Period, Year to Date, Targets, etc. Note: all elements may not be relevant or presented to all associates. Some associates may be eligible to participate in certain programs while others are not. A profile of each associate is contained in the system so the proper elements are presented. If an associate is not covered by a particular benefit or does not participate in a certain plan because of his or her job category, that element is not presented.

d. Messaging. Besides descriptions of the different elements and data presented, broader messages may be included on the statements or the online site. For example, messaging may be included to reinforce the value placed on associates and the employer's goal of offering compensation and benefits to recognize talent. A letter from a manager or company executive may be included. Some employers feel this message is actually most effective when it comes from someone who is known to the associates. This may not be the CEO. It might be a regional manager who is recognized as a leader by associates.

e. Assumptions and Disclaimers. Some employers like to list the assumptions associated with values appearing on statements and certain disclaimers. Such disclaimers might state the time periods being considered for certain elements. What's more, they might state that the data is for informational purposes and other agreements or documents that are in place relating to employment take precedent.

f. External links. Determine what links to other sites will be included. For instance, a link may be included to bring an associate directly to the web site of the company's 401(k) or health benefits plan administrator. Some employers include links to useful government sites, such as the Social Security Administration, where associates can get helpful data. Consider the site the "hub" of useful information relating to compensation, benefits and rewards. You might include a list of resources with phone numbers, e-mail addresses and web links. This makes the site a desired one-stop-shop for all pertinent information.

g. Importing Data from the HRIS. Importing data from the employer's System of Record – HRIS – is a key step when implementing an online Total Rewards Communication system. This is usually each employee's demographic data and details associated with their role. Attention is also given to updating the data on a regular schedule. Also, compensation information and other data can come from the HRIS.

h. Data Feeds and Interfaces. Data from 3rd Party Vendors. In some cases, an interface with a 3rd Party Vendor is used to bring data into the system following a standard file layout. Examples of vendors include: 401(k) Plan Sponsors, Health and Welfare Plan Administrators, Equity Award Managers, and other Benefits Providers.

i. Testing. Make sure all of the data is presented properly and statements or the online site looks great before going live. Of course, perform Quality Assurance testing to make sure the correct data is presented for the right associates. Besides testing for data accuracy, examine the usability, design, navigation and all other aspects of the TR Communication. Try it out on a small group and ask for their suggestions. Do they fully understand what is presented? Identify areas of confusion and address them before communicating with the full employee population.

j. Promotion of the TR Communication Statements or Online Site. Communicate with associates about the launch of the Total Rewards Communication and routinely remind associates about its value. Use company newsletters, flyers posted in the office, etc. Create some buzz.

k. Brand the site or statement. Give the statement or site a name so everyone can refer to it in the same way. Give it an identity. "Total Rewards Statement" is too bland.

l. Keep the content fresh and engaging. Consider using different people in the organization for help providing content. Changing content frequently is advised. Short new messages - just a few sentences - will help keep the site fresh and interesting. If you are using an online TR Communication, include videos and images and one or two question polls about relevant subjects (and then share the results.) Calculators and modeling tools can be appealing to associates. Keep it interesting and alive.

m. Analytics. Monitor traffic to the site to get a feel for what is working. Ask associates and managers for feedback. On the subject of analytics is personalizing messages with your Total Rewards Communication. Share messages that are relevant to associates and tie them to the information presented.

n. Ensure security and confidentiality. With the level of sensitive data associated contained in Total Rewards Communication, it is imperative that special consideration be given to security, privacy and confidentiality issues. Making sure access is limited to the right people and the proper content is being displayed are essential ingredients for success.

3: Give Managers Access to Cost Data

Frequently, managers do not have great clarity about the cost of benefits and other rewards provided for their direct reports. Total Rewards Communication addresses this shortcoming by bringing awareness about the costs of each program. As a result, it allows managers to more easily convey this information to members of their team.

This can be accomplished with a one-on-one meeting between the manager and each associate. In that session, there can be a review of:

- The elements available;
- Why they are supplied by the company;
- The associated value;
- How to participate in the benefit.

Such sessions can produce positive outcomes for both manager and associate. The manager is able to bring clear information to her team members about available rewards and benefits items. Consequently, this builds trust and engagement. For the associate, he or she will increase their understanding and appreciation of the programs and their full value.

In these meetings, it is not unusual to find situations where an employee did not know about the value of the employer paid portion of health insurance or other benefits. And there can be situations where an associate is eligible for a benefit, such as tuition reimbursement, but did not know it existed. Increased understanding and recognition of available benefits is a direct result of this communication effort.

Giving managers data about Total Rewards helps them become better leaders and to drive desired results for the organization.

4: Setting Your Goals: The Business Case

State you goals.   And have a plan to address those goals. This does not have to be elaborate.   But clarify up front what you want to accomplish with your Total Rewards Communication statements or online site.   In other words, make the business case.

This clarity of purpose will help in sharing the strategic and tactical elements in building your TR Communication. What are the number one and number two goals you are trying to achieve?   State them directly and let those goals be widely known throughout organization. Including managers from other departments in this process can build support for the TR Communication.

Some employers tie TR Communication to an organization's **Employee Value Proposition**, or EVP. Towers Watson, the human resource services and consulting firm, defines the Employee Value Proposition as: *"What is offered by an employer in exchange for the productivity and performance of an employee. It includes the entire employee "experience" from their rewards and benefits, to the opportunity for career development and also the more intrinsic elements of management style, work environment and culture."*

Simply put, "the give and the get."

According to research, organizations that do the most work developing and executing their Employee Value Proposition achieve superior financial performance over businesses with less-developed ones.

Following are examples for TR Communication goals stated by some employers we have worked with:

- Increase retention
- Upgrade the relationship between employer and employee
- Have employee better understand and appreciate the benefits provided
- Let employees know the amount of money paid by the company on their behalf for health benefits
- Support the alignment of efforts by associates with rewards
- Create awareness and get more people to participate in the 401(k) plan or other plans
- Build more engagement among employees
- Have associates understand more clearly how bonuses are earned and allocated: Pay-for-Performance
- Introduce more transparency in the rewards area
- Reinforce a culture of engagement
- Support employees throughout the employment life cycle
- Acknowledge contributions and recognize achievements
- Ensure that employees feel valued as employees

- Give managers greater understanding of the full value of employment and how to explain that to associates on their team.
- Show that the opportunities ahead can be valuable and rewarding.

5: Choosing the Elements

When designing the Total Rewards Communication solution to be used for associates, a critical phase is choosing what elements or "inputs" will be included and the categories for presenting those elements.

Breaking the TR Communication into logical sections will make the presentation easier for your employees. It will also help in organizing the design and data transfer of appropriate information. Consider what is important for you to emphasize. Make sure those elements are included first. (You can always add items later.)

WorldatWork, a global human resources association focused on compensation, benefits, work-life and integrated total rewards, created a framework for employers to consider. *Your Total Rewards Inventory*, a chart with the categories and examples of elements within each category, is shown on the following page. Quality information about many aspects of Total Rewards and the framework developed by WorldatWork is available at www.worldatwork.org.

The five reward categories in the WorldatWork framework can be used as the sections of a statement or pages used with an online Total Rewards Communication presentation. We are seeing a number of employers use this protocol, or a variation of it, in their design and communication of Total Rewards. The five categories in the framework are useful to build consistency and present data in an organized way. At the end of this Chapter we present the checklist of items to consider in these five categories:

a. Compensation
b. Benefits
c. Work-Life
d. Performance and Recognition
e. Development and Career Opportunities.

✓ **Compensation** covers Base Pay, Premium Pay and Variable Pay. Commissions and different bonuses and incentives are itemized.

✓ **Benefits** presents the value of the medical insurance plan and can show the employer and employee contributions. Life insurance and other health and welfare items can also be included: vision, dental, prescription, disability, etc. Retirement Plans, Social Security Insurance, Profit Sharing and other elements can fall under this category.

✓ **Work-Life** covers Maternity/Paternity Leave, Adoption Leave, Health and Wellness items, Nurse Line, Health Advocacy, Dependent Care, Community and Charitable Donation programs.

✓ **Performance and Recognition** can include information about awards, performance goals and specific programs for eligible employees. Sales achievements and other production-related metrics can be described here.

✓ **Development and Career Opportunities**. In this section, Learning, Tuition Reimbursement and Leadership Training are among the items to show. Employers can include links to available positions on their Career Site. Also, this section can have descriptions of other Career Development and Learning Information. The message is we want you to be successful and there are ways for you to advance your career goals and experience new and exciting things. Associates can find what is needed to be successful and what is offered to help learn and grow each step of the way.

Whether you follow the above framework or another one, it is important to give serious consideration to what elements will be included on your Total Rewards Communication.

One word of practical advice: We have seen employers struggle with trying to have every single element offered to employees included on their statement or site and getting bogged down in the fine details. As the saying goes, "sometimes the juice is not worth the squeeze."

In many cases it is better to capture the main items and not stress over having it totally comprehensive. A way to achieve this is to include the main items and then have a section that lists "Other Benefits" available to employers.

A list can suffice – even if the exact dollar value of these items is not displayed.

a. Compensation

Base Wages
- Salary Pay
- Hourly Pay
- Piece Rate Pay

Premium Pay
- Shift Differential Pay
- Weekend/Holiday Pay
- On-call Pay
- Call-In Pay
- Hazard Pay
- Bi-Lingual Pay
- Skill-Based Pay

Variable Pay
- Commissions
- Team-Based Pay

Bonus Programs

- Referral Bonus
- Hiring Bonus
- Retention Bonus
- Project Completion
- Bonus

Incentive Pay

Short-term:
- Profit Sharing
- Individual Performance Based Incentives
- Performance- Sharing Incentives

Long-term:
- Restricted Stock
- Performance Shares
- Performance Units
- Stock Options/Grants

b. Benefits

Legally Required/Mandated
- Unemployment Insurance
- Worker's Compensation Insurance
- Social Security Insurance
- Medicare
- State Disability Insurance (if applicable)

Health & Welfare
- Medical Plan
- Dental Plan
- Vision Plan
- Prescription Drug Plan
- Flexible Spending Accounts (FSAs)
- Health Reimbursement Accounts (HRAs)
- Health Savings Accounts (HSAs)
- Mental Health Plan
- Life Insurance
- Spouse/Dependent Life Insurance
- AD&D Insurance
- Short-Term/Long-Term Disability Insurance

Retirement
- Defined Benefit Plan
- Defined Contribution Plan
- Profit Sharing Plan
- Hybrid Plan

Pay for Time Not Worked

- Vacation
- Holiday
- Sick Leave
- Bereavement Leave
- Leaves of Absence (Military, Personal Medical, Family Medical)

c. Work-Life

Workplace Flexibility/ Alternative Work Arrangements

- Flex-Time
- Telecommuting
- Alternative Work Sites
- Compressed Workweek
- Job Sharing
- Part-time Employment
- Seasonal Schedules

Paid and Unpaid Time Off

- Maternity/Paternity Leave
- Adoption Leave
- Sabbaticals

Health and Wellness

- Employee Assistance Programs
- On-site Fitness Facilities
- Discounted Fitness Club Rates
- Weight Management Programs
- Smoking Cessation Assistance
- On-Site Massages
- Stress Management Programs
- Voluntary Immunization Clinics
- Health Screenings
- Nutritional Counseling
- On-Site Nurse
- Business Travel Health Services
- Disability Management
- Return to Work Programs
- Reproductive Health/ Pregnancy Programs
- 24-Hour Nurse Line
- On-Site Work-Life Seminars (Stress-Reduction, Parenting, etc.)
- Health Advocate

Community Involvement

- Community Volunteer Programs
- Matching Gift Programs
- Shared Leave Programs
- Disaster Relief Funds
- Sponsorships/Grants
- In-Kind Donations

Caring for Dependents

- Dependent Care Reimbursement Accounts
- Dependent Care
- Travel-Related Expense Reimbursements
- Dependent Care Referral and Resource Services
- Dependent Care Discount Programs or Vouchers
- Emergency Dependent Care Services
- Childcare Subsidies
- On-site Caregiver Support Groups
- On-Site Dependent Care
- Adoption Assistance Services
- After-School Care Programs
- College/Scholarship Information
- Scholarships
- Privacy Rooms
- Summer Camps & Activities
- Special Needs Childcare
- Disabled Adult Care
- Geriatric Counseling
- In-home Assessments for Eldercare

Financial Support

- Financial Planning Services and Education
- Adoption Reimbursement
- Transit Subsidies
- 529 Plans
- Savings Bonds
- Student Loan Assistance

Voluntary Benefits

- Long Term Care
- Auto/Home Insurance
- Pet Insurance
- Legal Insurance
- Identity Theft Insurance

- Employee Discounts
- Concierge Services
- Parking

Culture Change Initiatives

- Work Redesign
- Team Effectiveness
- Diversity/Inclusion Initiatives
- Women's Advancement Initiatives
- Work Environment Initiatives
- Multigenerational Initiatives

d. Performance and Recognition

Performance

- 1:1 Meetings
- Performance Reviews
- Project Completion/ Team Evaluations
- Performance Planning/ Goal Setting Sessions

Recognition

- Service Awards
- Retirement Awards
- Peer Recognition Awards
- Spot Awards
- Managerial Recognition Programs
- Organization-wide Recognition Programs
- Exceeding Performance Awards
- Employee of the Month/ Year Awards
- Appreciation Luncheons, Outings, Formal Events
- Goal-Specific Awards (Quality, Efficiency, Cost-Savings, Productivity, Safety)
- Employee Suggestion Programs

e. Development and Career Opportunities

Learning Opportunities

- Tuition Reimbursement
- Tuition Discounts
- Corporate Universities
- New Technology Training

- On-the-Job Learning
- Attendance at Outside Seminars and Conferences
- Access to Virtual Learning, Podcasts, Webinars
- Self-Development Tools

Coaching/ Mentoring

- Leadership Training
- Exposure to Resident Experts
- Access to Information Networks
- Formal or Informal Mentoring Programs

Advancement Opportunities

- Internships
- Apprenticeships
- Overseas Assignments
- Internal Job Postings
- Job Advancement/ Promotion
- Career Ladders and Pathways
- Succession Planning
- On/Off Ramps through Career Lifecycle
- Job Rotations

6: Design Phase

The TR Communication Statement or online site is an opportunity to convey important information to associates in a user friendly and visually appealing way. Having an exciting design is important, but it should not overshadow the content or make it difficult for employees to figure out what is being presented.

The associate experience is critical. Attention should be given to making it effortless and intuitive for associates to see and understand the content presented. To help give associates a positive experience and a proper understanding of the content presented use:

- Clear, short descriptions of all data;
- Plain language;
- A logical flow of information.

A great design can catch the attention of associates and present something new for employees. Total Rewards Communication can have a fresh look while still following corporate design standards – logos, fonts, colors, and graphics.

Below is a typical outline listing the sections that may be included in a TR Communication that may be helpful as a basic guide:

a. What it is. Introduction – What the TR Communication is about. The goals.

b. Why. Why the employer has generous compensation and benefits for associates.

c. Summary of the value of the elements presented. This can be presented in a table and in a chart, such as a pie chart showing the different items.

d. Sections for the elements and the associated financial values of items included in the TR Communication by category: (Compensation, Benefits, Work-Life, Performance and Recognition, Development and Career Opportunities.)

e. Modeling and Calculator features.

f. Resource List.

7: Messaging

When creating a Total Rewards Communication statement or online solution, most of the attention is on the numbers. That is, the dollar values associated with the various elements and aggregating those values to show the grand total. Yes, this is important. Yes, many associates just want to cut to the chase and see how much money they are getting. But there is more.

We see too little attention spent on the messaging that can be included with Total Rewards communication.

These are messages that support the Total Rewards items. On a printed or e-mailed statement, the messaging can show how the employer believes in its associates and wants to provide valuable benefits and competitive pay. The messaging can relate to the company's pay-for-performance culture. Certain benefits can be highlighted.

Messaging can be personalized for a group of employees. For example, a message presented to employees who are not enrolled in the company retirement plan might be about why saving for retirement is so important and explain the 401(k) enrollment process.

This is case specific for each employer, but messages about Total Rewards and why it is relevant to employees can support the goals established for the communication.

Dear Karen,

It's an exciting time to be a member of the Progress team. We greatly value the contribution you make to our company.

We recognize that you invest in the success of Progress every single day.

We believe it is important to offer you a competitive total rewards package that meets your expectations. This includes pay and innovative benefits that help you and your family members - now and in the future.

Thank you for helping us achieve our goals for the clients and the communities we serve.

Sincerely,
Robert J. Bascome
President and CEO

8: Assumptions and Disclaimers

In the previous Chapter we looked at messaging to be included for positive reinforcement of the Total Rewards supplied by an employer. Sometimes, employers care to include certain disclaimers or assumptions on their Total Rewards statements or online system relating to the content.

As part of the TR Communication development plan, include a step to have your attorney review the content. Too often employers ask for legal to review the site or document as the very last step in the roll out. Since it is not unusual for them to have some edits, it is best to learn about them sooner rather than later. It is easier to make changes to the content and the design early in the process.

Assumptions and Disclaimers may be included in the relevant section relating to the type of reward element to help put the values in their proper context.

To keep things simple, some employers include a general disclaimer at the end of the statement or on one page of the Total Rewards site. Of course, the idea is not to include a lot of legal wording but to help clarify what the associate sees.

A few examples are shown below to give some ideas of disclaimer wording that may be considered:

Assumptions

- Bonus compensation includes payments made for Calendar Year 2015.
- The cost of health and welfare benefits and insurance are for the latest period and may not reflect changes you have recently made to your coverage.
- Health and Welfare benefits have been calculated by annualizing premiums from the beginning of this year.
- Life insurance coverage and annualized premiums are based on the (Name of Insurance Company) records.
- The Retirement Savings Account amount shown includes any applicable rollovers and deferrals.

General Disclaimers

- This site does not constitute a contract of employment or a guarantee of benefits or future employment. In the event of conflict between this information and the official Plan documents, the Plan documents govern.

- Certain elements in this Total Rewards Communication are not guaranteed or fixed. Examples are bonus and incentive pay, continuing education and training. These elements vary and are based on specific circumstances.

- The pay and benefits information contained in this system reflect estimates based on your current compensation.

- This site represents a summary of data collected from a multitude of sources and is not intended to be the system of record. Any discrepancy between information reported in this system and the respective system of record is superseded by the system of record. The intent of this site is to be informational in nature. Projected future values do not carry any obligation to or guarantee any future compensation or benefits.

9: Links to Third Party Sites

Besides having current data available to associates, another benefit of an online site for TR Communication (versus a printed statement) is the ability to include useful links for employees. Including links on the site allows associates to seamlessly connect to third party plan administrators and other informative sites. This supports the TR Communication as the "go-to" place for everything related to rewards and benefits.

Links to plan administrators such as 401(k), health and welfare, equity administration, makes it easy for employees when they want to conduct a transaction with those providers. Using Single Sign On (SSO) technology makes it even simpler for employees by avoiding the need to remember various log-in credentials and passwords for each plan.

In an online version, or a printed statement, employers may consider including a list of resources along with the appropriate web site, e-mail and phone number for each.

This may be presented in a table format for easy reference.

Program	Who to Contact	Phone	Online
Human Resources	HR Department	800-555-8888	www.MyHRdept.net
Employee Assistance Program	Healthy Life	877-888-0000	www.HealthyLife.com
401(k) Plan	Fidelity Investments	800-343-3548	www.MyRetirement.com
Medical Insurance	Aetna	888-899-4221	www.aetna.com
Optional Group Life Insurance	MetLife	800-704-7287	www.myMetLife.com
Dental Insurance	Delta Dental	866-999-0000	www.deltadental.com
Disability	Aflac	800-444-0000	www.myaflac.com
Social Security	US Department of Social Security Administration	800-772-1213	www.socialsecurity.gov

10: Importing Data from the HRIS

After the employer decides what data elements will be shown on the TR Communication, the next step is determining the best source for each element.

Understanding where the data lives and how it can most efficiently travel to the TR Communication is a step in the configuration of the system or statement. This mapping exercise will often lead to the employer's Human Resource Information System (HRIS) or System of Record. Here is usually found the most current and accurate information about each employee.

With an online TR Communication system a feed from the HRIS will ensure that all current employees have access to the system. Established groups of employees who participate in certain benefits can also be kept up to date with data transferred from the HRIS.

A batch feed of data from the employer's HRIS once a day or once a week is common. The frequency for this import of data is determined being mindful that fresher data is more appealing to associates when presented in the end product.

When calculations are used to determine values to show to associates, the System of Record data is often the best source. Payroll deduction amounts for various benefits can also come from the HRIS.

When an employer uses an online TR system, data for presentation to associates can come from the employer's HRIS system, as described in the previous chapter. There may also be the desire to have certain data fed into the system from third party sources such as the 401(k) Plan Administrator.

In these cases, the employer or a vendor works with the third party company to agree on a common data file layout and schedule for the data transfer. Then the data is uploaded into the system for presentation to the proper associates. There are specifics to consider here. Such as: Does the employer want to show the total value of contributions to the associate's 401(k) account for a relevant period? Or, do you prefer to show a break-down of the amounts contributed to specific mutual funds within the account along with the total?

Another consideration when interfacing with third party vendors is the method of the data transfer. There are two basic ways. First is a batch process. This is where the vendor sends an updated batch of relevant data pertaining to associates on a set schedule to the employer's TR Communication system, usually a secure File Transfer Protocol (FTP) site. This might be done on a daily schedule that runs at 2 AM, for example. The data is then uploaded to the TR Communication system for presentation to associates. With this method, the data viewed by associates is fresh as of the close of business on the prior day.

An alternative is to have a dynamic connection with the vendor so the data presented is virtually real time. In this scenario, an associate is accessing the vendor's system with the employer's system as the gateway - and an identification and authentication process running in the background.

The batch method is generally preferred because there are fewer connectivity, error handling and monitoring issues involved.

Using the TR system as the central hub for fresh data can be of value to employees. The level of detail to display is considered in the design phase.

With some items, a formula to calculate the value to present on the TR Communication may be the right approach. Consider a company that offers certain employees a transportation allowance benefit that is equal to 2% of annual base salary. This amount can be determined with a simple computation and shown as a monthly, quarterly or annual amount which populates the relevant field for display to eligible associates.

Estimates can also be included as part of TR Communication. Of course, when estimates are used it should be clearly stated they are estimates and individual situations may vary.

For example, say an employer offers an on-site café where employees can purchase breakfast and lunch. An assumption can be made that the typical employee who uses this benefit will save $3 per meal compared with going to a local restaurant. If an employee uses the on-site café 4 times per week the savings = $12/week.   ($12/week x 50 weeks/year = $600 annual benefit.)

12: Testing and Using a Phase-In Approach

With a print or e-mail statement or an online TR Communication system, adequate time and resources must be allowed for thorough testing of the data and content. It sounds basic. But it is often overlooked.

The last thing anyone wants is to introduce a new exciting program and the data that is presented is wrong. Adequate testing and Quality Assurance reviews are necessary before the launch of a TR Communication.

A Pilot Phase may be useful. Select a small group of employees to preview their TR Statements or access the online site. Ask for their suggestions as part of a focus group and use their impressions and suggestions to make enhancements.

Some companies have deliberately started introducing the TR Communication to a sub-set of employees. This can have the effect of creating some buzz and more opportunities to draw attention to the program. The employer states "We are starting it with this group of employees and then adding other groups over time." As each new group is added another announcement can be made.

Think of it like the new movie that opens in selected cities, and then opens in more locations on different dates.

Besides the opportunity to shine a light on the TR Communication at different times, the phased in approach also gives the Project Team a chance to tweak and refine the product.

For those employers with a group of Human Resource Business Partners (HRBPs), these associates can be a terrific resource for testing and helping with the roll out.

13: Promotion of Total Rewards

Before the TR Communication is introduced to employees, thought should be given to how it will be promoted. Creating excitement and electricity is important in advance of the roll out and should continue on a regular basis. This is a critical part of the TR Communication project.

Rita Perkins, Principal with On Message Consulting in Milford, Ohio, specializes in employee communications. The following presentation is a guide Rita put together to point out some of the considerations relating to the communication of Total Rewards:

Communicating Total Rewards
By: Rita M. Perkins, Founder and Principal
On Message Consulting
1246 Spotted Fawn Run
Milford, OH 45150
Tel: 513-248-9824
www.onmessageconsulting.com

✓ **Communicating Total Rewards**
- A Solid Communication Campaign Draws Employees In

✓ **Total Rewards Statements are a powerful communication and planning tool.**
Ensure their success by:
- Peaking employee interest
- Providing the "WIIFM" for employees
- Helping employees access the site/statements and understand the data
- Continuing to draw employees back to the statements

✓ **It Starts With Planning**

✓ **STEP 1: Know Your Audience**
- Is it all employees or just a segment?
- Who is your "average" employee? What are the demographics?
- Can you send the same messages to everyone?
- Can you reach all employees the same way? Do you want to?
- Remember leaders, managers/supervisors and field HR

✓ **STEP 2: Plan Your Messages**
- What's In It For Me? (WIIFM)
- Retirement planning
- Financial planning

- Value/hidden paycheck from the Company

✓ **Where to find the tool and how to use it**
- Reinforce where they can find the tool
- Develop key messages on how to find/use the information

✓ **Creating Interest and "Buzz"**

✓ **Start with leader/management awareness**
- Introduce the Total Rewards Site to leaders, managers/supervisors and field HR
- Help them see the tool's power
- Provide talking points with key messages about the tool
- Ask for their help in promoting and reinforcing the tool

✓ **Create a campaign**
- Create your theme and stick with it
- Design it around a key message or WIIFM
- Posters provide quick, short visual messages
- Keep the message simple and the design clean
- Use electronic message boards to announce statements
- Email to associates announcing the Total Rewards Site
- Make it easy for employees by providing a link to the site and instructions on how to log in.

✓ **Create a campaign**
- Provide a print piece or online tutorial about the site
- Highlight the site's features and the information provided
- Don't forget about social media—Twitter and Facebook can help
- Staff kiosks in high traffic areas (cafeteria/break room) to increase interest and understanding

✓ **Sustaining the Momentum**

✓ **Maintaining interest over time is important**
- As an "evergreen" site, periodically remind employees to review their benefits on the site
- Keep information fresh -- update plan summary information with new messages

✓ **Find Ways to Maintaining interest**
- Look for logical reasons for people to go to the site. Examples might include:
  - o Open enrollment, to view their benefits
  - o Retirement planning at beginning of year
  - o 401(k) fund performance during the year

Announcement:

On-Line
Total Rewards
Communication

For Progress
Associates

August 1, 2017

*Members of the Progress Compensation and Benefits Team have been hard at work building a new web-based site – **Progress Rewards** - that will be introduced in August for associates.*

We will have access to this site to see information 24x7 about different Total Rewards items. Also, there are self-service tools on the site for associates, such as calculators for planning for retirement.   More details on how to access the site will be shared soon.

Announcing

New Progress Corporation Total Rewards Web Site for Associates

Launching
June 1, 2015

Please save the date!

Details to follow

Having everything available in one convenient place was the goal in designing this new site.

Out with the Old Files!

All of your Compensation and Benefits
Information in One place – On-line

Progress Corporation Employee Total Rewards Web Site

Introducing on-line access to current
information about compensation and
benefits.   All in one place, on-line.

The Total Rewards Site will be here on
June 1, 2015

<u>Re: *Introducing the New Total Rewards Communication Site*</u>

Dear Colleague,

It is a great pleasure to announce the introduction of our new Progress Total Rewards Web Site – **Progress Rewards** - on June 1, 2017.

We will now be able to conveniently find current information about compensation and benefits in one place. The site will be available 24x7, 365 days a year.   Access to the site will be through the Progress Employee Portal.

On the site you will find information about compensation, the value of your retirement plan, medical benefits information and much more. We know your life is not just about work. That is why we offer a comprehensive package that helps you grow personally and professionally, get rewarded for results and plan for your future.   We value you and your contributions to the success of Progress.

Our Human Resources and Compensation Teams have been working on this site for a number of months. They have come up with a spectacular site that is easy to navigate and will serve as the hub for information relating to Total Rewards.   Here's just a sample of what is available:

- Compensation & Benefits
- Medical, Dental and Vision Coverage
- 401(k) Information
- Insurance Coverages
- Employee Stock Purchase Program
- Self Service Calculators to See the Value of Employment

We hope you find this new site to be a valuable resource.

Sincerely,

Susan Walters

15: Branding and Naming

We always suggest giving the TR Communication Portal or Statement its own identity. Give it a name so everyone refers to it using the same title. That brand should evoke what the employer recognizes as the main purpose of the TR Communication.

Caesar's Entertainment, the casino operator with brands likes Harrah's and Caesar's Palace markets the "Total Rewards" brand extensively for their guest loyalty program. To stay clear of the gambling connotation, some employers avoid using the term Total Rewards entirely.

A list of ideas about naming TR Communication is shown below. Of course, the employer's brand can be included or it may relate to the employer's services or products. A car company might use "All Cylinders." A pizza maker might choose "The Whole Pie."

- My Wealth Statement
- My Personal Portfolio
- Value Summary
- Rewards Central
- Bravo!
- Value Statement
- Full Package
- My Compensation and Benefits Statement
- Rewards Hub
- Rewards Report
- Rewards Gateway
- My Rewards Planner
- My Rewards Summary
- Compensation and Benefits Package
- Total Compensation and Benefits Update
- My Rewards Report
- Rewards Corner
- Total Rewards 360

Associates want and expect to see fresh, relevant content. Without it, the TR Communication becomes boring and ignored. Just as promoting the TR Communication is critical when it is first introduced; keeping your audience's interest and enthusiasm requires thought and planning.

Managing TR Communication does not require you to be a creative writing expert. Just include relevant, timely information on your TR Communication. It can (and should) be brief. And remember to refer to your statement or site in other employee communications, such as newsletters and announcements.

Short, interesting pieces that support the goals of the TR communication can be inserted at the beginning of the TR Communication – an introductory letter or message from a manager. Then, the statement-type information and the values follow.

Company news, updates from plan sponsors, excerpts or links to financial and retirement planning blogs or articles can all be used. Reminders about key dates are also worth including: open enrollment deadlines, tax form delivery dates, performance review dates.

"Mini-interviews" with company leaders on relevant topics are easy to develop. The interview can be conducted by e-mail. For example, send an e-mail with a few questions to a leader and request brief responses for inclusion in the TR Communication: *What do you think is something our associates often don't understand about our benefit plans? What is your advice about retirement savings?*

Personalization can also be used to deliver specific messages for certain groups of employees. If a particular department has achieved success with a project or a community service project, it can be recognized in the appropriate section of the TR Communication.

Employers have found that communicating the "Total Offer" to job candidates can be an effective recruiting tool. A Total Rewards Statement for the position under consideration can be developed following the basic framework of the statement used to communicate with current employees.

If an employer uses an on-line Total Rewards site, candidates can be given a link to view their proposed Total Offer on-line. An example is shown on the following page.

This helps candidates understand the full value of a position and make a fair evaluation of the job. In some situations the base salary may be equal of even lower than other positions being considered but other reward elements can bring the full value to a higher level. Consider the employer 401(k) match, profit sharing and other available benefits for inclusion in the Total Rewards Offer.

This is not meant to replace the formal Offer Letter given to candidates. The Offer Letter usually provides details about the position, schedule, and other terms and conditions. The Total Offer communication is focused on the full value of potential employment and can be effective in the recruiting process.

Dear Kim,

We appreciate your considering joining the Progress Corporation team.

At Progress, we recognize that associates are critical to everything we do. We are committed to offering a Total Rewards package that attracts and retains associates who are engaged, energized and innovative.

If you join Progress, your Total Rewards will include compensation, health and retirement benefits, learning opportunities and other valuable items. A summary of the major elements (and the estimated annualized value) you would receive in the position - **Senior Project Planner** – is shown here. Since we do not know your preference in terms of selecting health insurance, please use one of the following values as an estimate for the value of this item, if you elect coverage:

- Individual Coverage $ 7,000 per year
- Individual + 1 $ 9,000 per year
- Family Coverage $12,000 per year

These are estimates and we look forward to reviewing this with you in further detail.

My Total Offer – Kim Smith	Annualized Amount
My Direct Compensation	$ 80,000
My Benefits – Health	Insert value from above
My Benefits – Retirement 401(k)	$ 5,000
My Work Life	$ 4,750
My Performance	$ 8,242
My Career	$ 3,500
Totals	$ 101,492

Sincerely,

George Wilkinson

18: Total Rewards Communication in Mergers

What does this merger or acquisition mean to me? That question is commonly top of mind for employees when companies are sold or combine in an M&A transaction.

Managers can use Total Rewards Communication to address important issues being considered by associates in an organized manner. At the same time, employers will gain credibility by being inclusive and caring. Having a levelheaded, thoughtful approach to employee matters at sensitive times, such as with an acquisition, can go a long way. There is always a great deal of speculation and gossip about the fallout of M&A. Using Total Rewards communication can cut through at least some of this and help set the record straight.

There are certainly situations where all of the compensation and benefits decisions following a merger or other transaction are not fully known out of the gate. But there are always some of the elements that have been worked through. And these are the ones that can be communicated. It is okay to say that some items are still being reviewed by management and more information will be shared later.

Some of the items that can be addressed include:

- Will the pay structure of the acquiring company and the company being acquired be combined?

- Will the different structures be maintained for a period of time? If so, how long?

- What happens to the health and welfare plans and other benefits of each company?

- What about the 401(k) or other retirement savings plans of each company?

- What does an employee have to do in terms of rewards and benefits enrollment?

- Are plan administrators being changed?

- Who is in charge of HR and benefits?

- How can I get answers to my questions?

A merger or acquisition can be a value inflection point for a company. Proper communication with employees about critical information – including rewards – can make a profound difference in these situations.

After you have introduced the Total Rewards Communication, ask associates frankly what they like, what they don't like and what they want to see added or replaced as part of the process.

We discussed the importance of having an advance communication to let associates know a TR Communication is coming and its purpose. After the site or statement is launched, it is a good practice to have a survey to seek feedback and learn how the TR Communication was received.

To see if there are any changes in views toward TR Communication over time, consider surveying a sample of employees monthly for the first six months after the go-live date.

With an online site, it is easy to see traffic to the Total Rewards Communication pages. Standard analytics are usually included so the administrator can see what pages get the most attention and where employees spend the most time.

If there are pages that get little traffic, either associates don't know they are there – or they are not interesting. Of course, this allows the employer to promote the low traffic pages or remove them.

With an online TR Communication, reporting and data analytics are possible. Since the system is tracking relevant data, management reports about the enrollment level in particular benefits can be produced, as an example. This can be organized by group, such as job category, location or division, to identify where attention might be needed. Trends and other correlations can be recognized.

TR Communication can be used to give employees an easy way to see the full economic value of employment today **and** model their potential future value, based on certain assumptions. The variables or assumptions are made by an employee to create a personalized model.

Christopher Ford, a thought leader and HR and IT executive in the San Francisco Bay Area, calls this the ***Walk Away Value***. The concept is to put the model out there in a forthright way, right at the fingertips of associates and their managers. And let associates judge the value of employment. It helps answer the question on the mind of every associate: *Is this position going to meet my expectations over the next few years?*

Why not recognize that and provide the tools to associates as part of the Total Rewards Communication?

Walk Away Value is the amount of money you are leaving behind if you separate from your current employer. When considering another position, it lets the associate understand exactly what they are walking away from (based on certain financial assumptions.)

According to Christopher Ford, "Walk Away Value also creates a long term engagement connection with employees. When employees think about leaving a company for better compensation, they tend to think about total compensation at a point in time. An employee who realizes their Walk Away Value thinks about Total Rewards vs. Total Compensation, and thinks about a period of time (3 to 5 years) versus a point in time. Walk Away Value could become a powerful retention tool in the marketplace."

The online tool presents a standard list of reward elements to the associate. Then it builds a model showing the estimated future value (usually 3 or 4 years) of those elements and their sum, based on assumptions about growth made by the employee.

The model is easy for employees to use. It works like this:

1. Take your current compensation, incentive awards and other reward items such as company paid benefits and profit sharing.

2. Apply a growth factor to these items. (Salary increase, Appreciation of stock value associated with RSU's or Option Grants, etc.)

3. Aggregate the value of these items looking ahead 3, 4 or 5 years.

4. The sum is the Walk Away Value.

The result can be eye-opening.

Walk Away Value Modeling

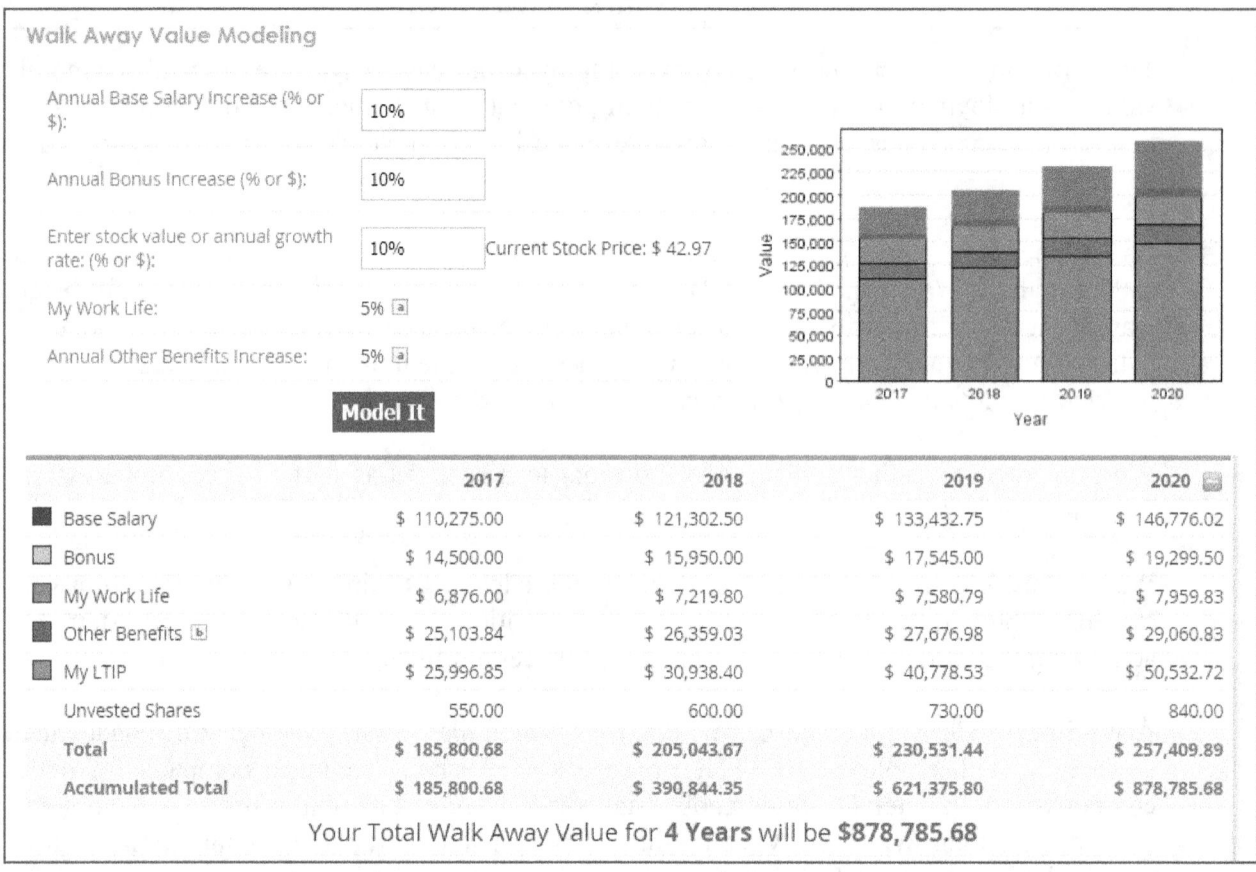

Annual Base Salary Increase (% or $):	10%
Annual Bonus Increase (% or $):	10%
Enter stock value or annual growth rate: (% or $):	10% Current Stock Price: $ 42.97
My Work Life:	5% [a]
Annual Other Benefits Increase:	5% [a]

Model It

	2017	2018	2019	2020
Base Salary	$ 110,275.00	$ 121,302.50	$ 133,432.75	$ 146,776.02
Bonus	$ 14,500.00	$ 15,950.00	$ 17,545.00	$ 19,299.50
My Work Life	$ 6,876.00	$ 7,219.80	$ 7,580.79	$ 7,959.83
Other Benefits [b]	$ 25,103.84	$ 26,359.03	$ 27,676.98	$ 29,060.83
My LTIP	$ 25,996.85	$ 30,938.40	$ 40,778.53	$ 50,532.72
Unvested Shares	550.00	600.00	730.00	840.00
Total	**$ 185,800.68**	**$ 205,043.67**	**$ 230,531.44**	**$ 257,409.89**
Accumulated Total	**$ 185,800.68**	**$ 390,844.35**	**$ 621,375.80**	**$ 878,785.68**

Your Total Walk Away Value for **4 Years** will be **$878,785.68**

21: What Should Not Be Included?

There is information that should **not** be shown on Total Rewards Statements or communications.

Of course, this is employer specific. But information that is considered sensitive and confidential to your business or anything that is of a highly competitive nature should be carefully reviewed and not presented in the TR Communication.

For example, an employer in the auto industry should not include the cost the employer pays for employee benefits per car (production unit.) This could wind up in the hands of a competitor and is not necessary to include in the TR Communication anyway.

Sometimes the question arises about content that is available somewhere else. *If it can be found elsewhere should it be repeated on the TR Communication?* We believe the answer can be yes.

Remember that the TR Communication is seen as the "hub" for relevant content by associates. Even if information is available somewhere else, there is a convenience factor in having it included on the TR Communication. So rather than searching for a document or User ID and Password relating to a benefit supplied, it can be presented neatly in the TR Communication.

For employers with global operations, there is generally a desire to have the Total Rewards Communication available to international employees as well as those in the United States. In doing this, the employer must give consideration to the different data elements that may be relevant to associates in each country.

For example, health benefits may be closely associated with employment in the US, but this is not the case in many other nations. So including health benefits on the statement would not be considered a benefit related to employment. Associates would probably not see that as a valuable item connected to the employer. On the other hand, employees may receive transportation allowances and meal subsidies in certain countries that are closely tied to employment.

Beyond compensation data, the general rule many employers follow is to display in the TR Communication those rewards that are supplied by the employer and are above what is automatically available to everyone, even if they are not an employee.

In addition to deciding what elements to include on the TR Communication, identifying where the data is found for international associates may require attention. It may not be the case that all the data is consolidated neatly in the employer's central, primary HRIS. There may be multiple payroll or HRIS systems and third parties, such as insurance brokers or agents may be the source of certain data elements. With an organized approach, the appropriate data elements and their sources can be identified and configured for presentation to a company's associates.

23: Mobility

If an online TR communication solution is being deployed for employees, it is essential that the site is designed with the ability to present data for associates when using mobile devices within or outside of the office.

Using a Responsive Web Design (RWD) allows for viewing of content on tablets, smart phones and other mobile devices. RWD is used to ensure easy reading and navigation with a minimum of resizing, panning, and scrolling across a wide range of devices.

Associates will expect the system to be accessible and present properly on their iPads and other devices so attention should be given to this as part of the project scope.

For employers, supplying an optimal viewing experience across a wide range of devices will enhance overall satisfaction and increase traffic.

If using a vendor for the design or hosting of the TR Communication, be sure to ask about mobility capabilities supported by the system.

24: Security and Confidentiality

By its very nature, every TR communication is highly confidential.

Security considerations must be a part of the planning process. If statements are e-mailed, they should always be encrypted.

With an online TR Communication solution, security considerations include application-level encryption and decryption algorithms to protect sensitive information.

Tushar Ghoshal, our colleague and Chief Technology Officer with HRsoft, supplied a more technical review of considerations relating to IT security for TR Communication:

> The Information Technology system used should have application level encryption and decryption. All sensitive information should be encrypted. Connections established through SSL should be used for transmittal of sensitive information. It is also recommended to deploy DMZ(s), Stateful Application Firewalls that inspect packets, authentication and single sign on, layers of Internal Firewalls with Network Intrusion Detection/Prevention (IDS/IPS), access control (ACL) and round the clock monitoring. Security for outside elements can be covered by a combination of SSO (Single Sign-On) and external firewall solutions.
>
> Access to data should be further restricted by Authorization via Roles, Permissions and Business Hierarchy driven Data Validations. Dynamic/Proactive Security Scans must be run periodically to ensure all security measures in place are tested.
>
> Administrators who have rights to access the system must be trained to have a clear understanding about the confidential nature of the data and to treat all such information on a need-to-know basis.

As part of the TR Communication planning process the technology department plays an active role.

Working together with IT, security and confidentiality issues are identified and addressed. As system updates and changes are made, IT will make the necessary adjustments to the site so it continues to meet all requirements.

25: Summary

We set out to explore ways Total Rewards Communication can be brought to an organization and create value for both employers and employees. In doing so, we have looked at a number of fundamental issues along with some ideas, tips and hints.

Information is powerful. And communication is powerful.

Total Rewards Communication goes to the heart of what an employer stands for and the relationship with associates.

An effective TR Communication program can be a terrific way to help employers and employees achieve success.

Please share your experience, impressions and suggestions with us.

Appendix 1: Sample Pages of a Total Rewards Site

Summary Page

My Total Rewards Summary · My Direct Compensation · My Benefits · My Retirement Plans · My Work Life · My Performance

WAVE

One of our goals of being a great place to work is to connect you to resources and opportunities for every stage of your life and career. Whether you have an immediate need or a long-term goal, your employee benefits and the additional resources we offer are designed to make life better now and in the future.

If you need any additional details on how to use your benefits and HR policy information you can also click the Knowledge Center link on the top right of this page. This self-service solution is your online resource for all HR and work-life questions.

Thank you, for all your contributions!
Eva Chen
Chief Executive Officer and Co-founder

My Direct Compensation

COMPENSATION TYPE	2017 TARGET	YEAR-TO-DATE	LAST YEAR
My Direct Compensation	$ 124,956	$ 39,375	$ 134,001
My Benefits	$ 36,046	$ 13,517	$ 32,696
My Work Life	$ 16,273	$ 6,876	$ 250
My Performance	$ 15,500	$ 500	$ 11,725
TOTALS	$ 192,775	$ 60,268	$ 178,672

Compensation Page

My Total Rewards Summary · **My Direct Compensation** · My Benefits · My Retirement Plans · My Work Life · My Performa

WAVE

We understand how talented and critical you are to the success of the organization. In line with your contributions the organization offers a competitive direct compensation package including salary, bonus, company performance bonus and virtual shares. Based upon your performance you will also be offered the opportunity to receive competitive pay increases, bonus and equity awards to keep you and your organization account growing as we continue to grow with you. As we succeed financially, so too will you.

Mahendra Negi, Chief Finance Officer

My Total Compensation

COMPENSATION TYPE	2017 TARGET	YEAR-TO-DATE	LAST YEAR
Base Salary	$ 105,000	$ 38,550	$ 100,250
Commission	$ 17,500	$ 500	$ 14,500
MBO	$ 2,456	$ 325	$ 4,251
Retention	$ 0	$ 0	$ 10,000
Relocation	$ 0	$ 0	$ 5,000
MY TOTAL COMPENSATION	$ 124,956	$ 39,375	$ 134,001

Benefits Page

Setting you up for long-term health and financial well-being is important to us. With our well-rounded and in many cases industry leading benefits offerings this has never been easier. Matching 401K contributions, numerous health and dental plan offerings, health care savings accounts, counseling services, life insurance benefits, generous paid time off are only some of the ways we strive to protect and foster your health and financial well-being now and far into the future. With us your pay goes well beyond your paycheck!

Virginia White, EVP Employee Benefits

My Combined Benefits

BENEFIT TYPE	2017 TARGET	YTD EMPLOYER PORTION	YTD MY PORTION	LAST YEAR EMPLOYER PORTION
401(k)	$ 4,040	$ 6,500	$ 3,100	$ 3,838
Health & Welfare Plans	$ 4,550	$ 3,004	$ 1,396	$ 4,322
My Defined Benefit Pension	$ 4,200	$ 5,500	$ 0	$ 3,990
Paid Time Off	$ 3,950	$ 3,250	$ 0	$ 3,752
State and Federal Insurances	$ 7,150	$ 6,850	$ 4,307	$ 6,792
TOTALS	$ 23,890	$ 25,104	$ 8,803	$ 22,696

Work-Life

Your well-being is centered in a balanced life. We are very mindful of the value of your family and your personal time and strive to offer flexible work-life benefits and programs that reflect and enrich your life in and away from the office. We are leading the charge in helping reshape the modern busy workforce. We hope that you continue to enjoy being a part of our family in and out of the office and we will continue to offer you the opportunity to lead a balanced and satisfying life.

Bob Kedrosky, Sr. Director - Human Resources

Work Life Programs

PROGRAM NAME	2017 TARGET	YTD EMPLOYER PORTION	YTD MY PORTION
Child Care Allowances	$ 4,500	$ 2,300	$ 0
Employee Assistance Program	$ 2,800	$ 1,500	$ 0
Home Office Reimbursement	$ 850	$ 250	$ 0
Matching Gift Programs	$ 1,623	$ 526	$ 0
Wellness Programs	$ 6,500	$ 2,300	$ 0
TOTALS	$ 16,273	$ 6,876	$ 0

401(k) Calculator – Here an associate would enter certain values relating to contribution level and employer match to model the growth potential of their account.

Instructions:

"Enter all of the fields below, then press the **View Schedule** button."

Note:

1. Contributions are made at the end of the period.
2. The maximum pre-tax amount that you are allowed to contribute to this plan is capped annually by the IRS. Therefore, the cap may change annually. This calculator will not check to see if you are over-contributing! That is a function of your plan administrator. It is more complicated than setting a $16,500 (pre-tax) limit on contributions (the limit for 2011). Your plan may have its own (lower) limits - or allow after-tax contributions. The IRS has also set limits on the total amount you may contribute to your 401(k) from all sources in a given year, including employer match or profit-sharing contributions and any employee after-tax contributions.
3. Due to rounding, the calculations are approximate and intended to be used only as a guide.

Current 401(k) Balance:	$ 85000	
Current Annual Income:	$ 43000	
Expected Annual Salary Increase:	4 %	
Percent of Salary Withheld for 401(k):	5 %	Invested Annually
Employer Match Annually:	%	
Employer maximum:	4 %	of your salary
Years to Fund 401(k):	15	
Average Annual Interest Rate Earned:	6 %	

View Schedule

401(k) Calculator Output Schedule – Shows the projected balance for each year in a future period based on the variables entered.

401(k) Contribution Schedule

Fund 401(k) for 15 years
Annual Income of $ 43,000.00 increasing 4% per year
Beginning Balance = $ 85,000.00
Contribute 5% of Salary
Your Employer will match up to 4% of Salary
Annual Interest Rate = 6%

YEAR #	BEGINNING BALANCE	YOU CONTRIBUTE	EMPLOYER CONTRIBUTES	EARNINGS	ENDING BALANCE
2017	$ 85000.00	$ 2150.00	$ 1720.00	$ 5100.00	$ 93970.00
2018	$ 93970.00	$ 2236.00	$ 1788.80	$ 5638.20	$ 103633.00
2019	$ 103633.00	$ 2325.44	$ 1860.35	$ 6217.98	$ 114036.77
2020	$ 114036.77	$ 2418.46	$ 1934.77	$ 6842.21	$ 125232.20
2021	$ 125232.20	$ 2515.20	$ 2012.16	$ 7513.93	$ 137273.49
2022	$ 137273.49	$ 2615.80	$ 2092.64	$ 8236.41	$ 150218.34
2023	$ 150218.34	$ 2720.44	$ 2176.35	$ 9013.10	$ 164128.23
2024	$ 164128.23	$ 2829.25	$ 2263.40	$ 9847.69	$ 179068.58